Original title:
The Ocean's Endless Song

Copyright © 2025 Creative Arts Management OÜ
All rights reserved.

Author: Hugo Fitzgerald
ISBN HARDBACK: 978-1-80587-300-6
ISBN PAPERBACK: 978-1-80587-770-7

The Blues of a Brine-soaked Chorus

A fish in a tux sings with flair,
While jellyfish float without a care.
Crabs tap dance on a sandy stage,
Making waves with the latest rage.

Seagulls squawk in a comic tone,
As they steal snacks and munch on scone.
A starfish claims it's a movie star,
But can't quite remember just who they are.

Dolphins chuckle, doing flips in glee,
They pull off pranks while sipping tea.
A whale sings deep, tries to sound cool,
But all their tunes make the fishly drool.

Under the waves, it's a riot of sound,
With laughter and splashes all around.
They all join in on a wild refrain,
In this salty world, joy's never in vain.

The Muse of the Mariner

A sailor sings a jolly tune,
As gulls dance under a silver moon.
His compass spins in a fit of glee,
Claiming a treasure, a bright green pea.

He charts the course with a wink and grin,
While fish sneak by with a wink and swim.
The waves chuckle as they slip and slide,
His mismatched socks, a source of pride!

Waves Unfurling Ancient Tales

The waves are storytellers in disguise,
With splashes of laughter, they rise and rise.
They whisper secrets of ships gone wild,
And dolphins that dance like an excited child.

A surfer in shorts, oversize and bright,
Rides a wave that's nearly out of sight.
He shouts with joy, "I'm a sea star!"
But crashes down, just shy of the bar!

Cadences of Blue Waters

In the blue depths where the seaweed sways,
A crab plays the banjo, oh what a craze!
He strums and he plucks with living flair,
While fish form a chorus, beyond compare!

The octopus joins in with a dance,
While turtles try hard to keep up with the chance.
They waltz in circles, with laughter and cheer,
Claiming, "We've got the moves, bring on the beer!"

Lapping Limn of the Far Horizon

The sun paints pictures on water's face,
Where seagulls compete in a wacky race.
They flap and they flop, quite a silly sight,
As they gossip about the stars at night.

A sandcastle king proclaims very loud,
"If I rule the sand, I'll make you all proud!"
But a wave comes sneaking, with a giggly glee,
And washes away his grand legacy!

Serenade of Waves at Dusk

When the sun dips low and sea birds croon,
The crabs start dancing, oh what a tune!
With flip-flops flying, we join in the fun,
Splashing each other while we try to run.

The fishy band plays an off-key set,
While jellyfish twirl, not a single regret!
Surfers are giggling, they've lost their way,
Riding foam mountains, they shout 'Hip-hip-hooray!'

Lament of the Starry Deep

Beneath the stars in the watery swirl,
Octopuses grumble as they twist and twirl.
They want a spotlight, a role in a play,
But their ink spills out in a messy ballet.

The clams roll their eyes, they just can't believe,
That fish find it funny, weep without reprieve.
While dolphins are chuckling, tales all unfold,
Of treasure maps lost and shrimp that were bold.

Melodies from the Abyss

In the deep dark blue, where the strange things roam,
Mermaids are singing, but it sounds like foam.
With bubbles and giggles, they serenade night,
While eels do the shimmy, oh what a sight!

The snails bring the snacks, in a shell-inspired way,
They host a grand feast at the end of the day.
With seaweed confetti and kelp on the side,
They toast to their antics, with laughter and pride.

Dance of Salt and Foam

On the sandy shores, where the gulls go 'caw',
Seagulls are strutting, they've got some good law.
They strike silly poses, with flair and delight,
While waves keep on crashing, a comical fight.

With sandcastle armies, they're ready to clash,
The crabs march forward, do they have any sass?
The tide breaks a line, with a splash and a cheer,
It's a playful adventure, no worries, no fear!

Whispers of the Tidal Breeze

A fish wore a hat, oh what a sight,
He danced with the crabs, late into the night.
Seagulls were laughing, circling so high,
As a dolphin did cartwheels, under the sky.

The clams held a party, what a big scene,
With cocktails of seaweed and jellybean.
Octopus DJ spun some groovy old tunes,
While starfish did breakdances under the moons.

Currents of Celestial Harmony

A turtle in shades slicked back his hair,
While shrimp did the limbo without any care.
The whale chimed in with a bass guitar,
As jellyfish twinkled like little bright stars.

The crabs formed a band, called 'Claw and Aye',
With clams singing backup—oh me, oh my!
They rocked the sea floor, a true ocean show,
While seaweed waved on, just going with the flow.

Echoes Beneath the Blue

An octopus juggled some fish in a row,
While seahorses raced, moving fast but so slow.
The stingrays were gliding, as smooth as can be,
With turtles in tow—oh, look at them flee!

They played hide and seek, in coral so bright,
The grouper was 'it' with a laugh oh so light.
As bubbles popped loudly, they all laughed and cheered,
While the underwater world shined, undeterred.

Rhythms of the Surfing Tide

A wave caught a seal with a surfboard in paws,
As crabs shouted 'righteous', cheering his cause.
With each wipeout, the fishes did giggle,
A sight to behold, all wiggly and wiggle.

A porpoise named Larry gave tricks a sweet spin,
While anglerfish flashed with their light-up grin.
They rode every swell, in a jolly parade,
Laughter and splashes, a grand ocean charade!

Soliloquy of the Seas

The fish hold a meeting, oh what a sight,
Trying to solve who's the best swimmer tonight.
With fins all a-flutter, they giggle and splash,
While crabs in the corner just make a loud crash.

The seagulls join in with a sarcastic squawk,
Debating if seaweed is better than rock.
The waves play along with their frothy applause,
As dolphins do tricks, and they all give a pause.

Harmony in the Depths

Beneath the blue surface, where sea creatures dwell,
A clam tells a story that's hard to expel.
He giggles at oysters, who sit in their shells,
While shrimp laugh aloud at their funny fish smells.

Octopus gets fancy, with ink he does write,
A poem for starfish, who can't hold on tight.
With laughter and bubbles, they dance in the foam,
Creating a ruckus in their watery home.

Tidal Serenades

The tides roll in dance, with a skip and a hop,
As a lobster starts singing, it just can't be stopped.
He cracks all his jokes while the jellyfish float,
Enjoying the rhythm, they wiggle and gloat.

Crabs form a conga, and seahorses sway,
In a musical sea where the sea turtles play.
With bubbles as beats, they all sing along,
To the quirky, wild chorus of this underwater throng.

Oceanic Echoes at Dusk

As the sun starts to dip and the sea turns to gold,
A whale hums a tune that's delightfully bold.
With fishes as backup, they bellow and croon,
Making echoes of laughter beneath the soft moon.

Starfish can't clap but they still bring the cheer,
With a twirl and spin, oh they're truly sincere.
The waves join the chorus with a splash and a sing,
In a twilight performance, they all twine and swing.

Glistening Tides and Moonlit Dreams

Waves crash in a funny arc,
Seagulls squawk like a barking lark.
Flippers flop and dolphins dance,
Underneath the moon's bright glance.

Crabs in suits do waddle by,
With tiny ties, they look quite spry.
They hold a party on the shore,
Eager for the tide to pour.

Surfboards slide, the jokers glide,
As salty waves become their ride.
With shouts and splashes filled with cheer,
The ocean's laugh you can still hear.

Lost flip-flops roam like tiny ships,
In search of toes for some sweet trips.
With every tumble, giggles soar,
Adventures linger forevermore.

Harmony of Shell and Sand

A crab in shades, a clam with flair,
Finding treasures here and there.
Seashells gossip as they lie,
Winking at each passerby.

Starfish sing a silly tune,
As jellyfish float by like balloons.
Sandcastles built with great delight,
Soon washed away by a comical sight.

Gulls argue over the best snack,
With fishy jokes and a loud clack.
The seaweed sways, it sways so bright,
Dancing under the sun's warm light.

Tide pools hold a secret show,
Where tiny fish put on a glow.
Each splash a laugh, each ripple fun,
Nature's jest has just begun.

Ballad of the Wayward Sailor

A sailor bold, with a floppy hat,
Lost his map while chasing a cat.
He sails in circles, what a sight,
Sunburned skin, but heart's so light.

Fish parade beneath his boat,
While seagulls try to steal his oat.
"Yo ho!" he shouts, "I'm quite the chap!"
But his snacks end up in the sea's lap.

Mermaids giggle, hear them sing,
As waves respond with a splashy fling.
He swabs the deck, but slips again,
Spinning like the wildest hen.

Chasing dreams across the foam,
He finds that the sea's his second home.
With every bob and twist he makes,
The ocean laughs, his heart just quakes.

Chant of the Rising Tide

The tide rolls in with a bouncy beat,
It tickles toes with a fizzy greet.
Sand slips under, what a charade,
Footprints vanish, then they wade.

Seashells play hide-and-seek at dawn,
As crabs plot pranks till the sun is gone.
Bluefish swim in a slapdash race,
While turtles grin with a leisurely pace.

Frothy bubbles giggle in sync,
Matching the sailors who slurp their drink.
The surf sings songs of silly glee,
While children splatter their feet with spree.

Each wave brings laughter, each splash a cheer,
A symphony of joy that rings so clear.
For the ocean's blend of fun and tide,
Is a quirky dance we can't let slide.

A Symphony of Waters

Little fish dance in the waves,
Making tunes with silly braves.
Crabs get groovy on the sand,
Clapping claws, it's quite unplanned.

Seagulls soar, a funny sight,
Singing off-key, taking flight.
Jellyfish join with a bounce,
While the seaweed sways, they pounce.

Turtles shuffle, kicking sand,
Waltzing to a song so grand.
Starfish giggle, stuck in place,
Trying hard to keep the pace.

Splashing waves, a chorus loud,
Making music, proud and bowed.
Underwater, the fun's a blast,
In this symphony, we laugh fast.

Whispers of the Distant Shore

The tide rolls in with a cheerful grin,
Whispering secrets with a playful spin.
Seashells chat, gossiping away,
While sand crabs dance, they love to sway.

The beach ball hops with joyful glee,
Bouncing high, then splashing free.
Wind tugs gently at each sun hat,
As kids run by, all squirting a cat.

A dolphin leaps, a graceful clown,
Making waves, it's ocean's renown.
Seagulls squawk with a snarky tone,
As beachgoers munch on ice cream cones.

Waves tickle toes, oh what a treat,
A funny jig with each silly beat.
Chasing foam and laughter's flare,
The whispers of fun fill the salty air.

A Rhythmic Retreat into Blue

The surf's a dance, a bubbly spree,
Where fish practice their choreography.
Octopuses twirl in the current's sway,
While sea cucumbers chill in their bay.

Pelicans dive with a comical splash,
Looking for fish in a chaotic dash.
Starfish claps with no hands to spare,
As bubbles rise high, floating in air.

Sea horses strut in a goofy parade,
Snapping photos of their escapade.
Kelp sways gently, a green-faced cheer,
For every wave brings a laugh and a cheer.

The backdrop hums in playful delight,
As sunsets paint the sky a bright light.
In this rhythm, the blues run deep,
Where smiles linger and laughter keeps.

Water's Wondrous Whisper

Raindrops fall, a playful tap,
Making puddles for a giggling flap.
Frogs croak songs of silly times,
While fish sing along in watery rhymes.

Bubbles rise like little jokes,
Making waves from all the folks.
Seals juggle shells, a comical feat,
In the splash zone, here's where we meet.

Crabs march sideways to the beat,
In their own shoes, it's quite the feat.
Mermaids giggle, flipping their hair,
Making waves without a care.

The current hums with a tickling tune,
While dusk arrives under a silver moon.
In this place where laughter flows,
Water's whispers are where fun grows.

The Lament of the Lost Surfers

There once were some surfers quite bold,
Who chased after waves, dreams untold.
But boards went afloat, oh what a shame,
They swam back to shore, feeling quite lame.

With sunscreen and snacks, they took to the sand,
Dreaming of waves far too grand.
But the tide had a sense of its own, you see,
It pulled all their snacks right out to the sea!

They yelled and they cheered for a wave to ride,
But the waves just laughed and pushed them aside.
No trophies or glory, just soggy hair,
And tales of the waves they forgot to compare.

Now they sit on the shore in a lovely display,
With seagulls that steal their lunch every day.
They ponder their fate with a chuckle and sigh,
As the ocean keeps laughing at all those who try.

Stories Carried by the Tide

Once a bottle set sail on a quest,
Filled with tales, it thought it was best.
But on the shore, it met a crab,
Who stole it away in a furious jab!

"Hey, what's this?" asked the crab with a grin,
"Can I read your tales? Where do I begin?"
The bottle just bobbed, slightly embarrassed,
As seagulls squawked and the tide harassed.

The bottle was shaky, a little confused,
As crabs, they danced, and flopped, and amused.
Stories of pirates and ships made of gold,
Turned into jokes as the tide flowed bold.

Each wave carried laughter, tales of delight,
While the crab cracked the lid with one powerful bite.
The bottle sighed out tales, instead of the woes,
Making friends in the sea, where the soft laughter flows.

Hymn of the Tempest

In the midst of a storm, the sailors did cheer,
As wind whipped their beards and tossed back their beer.
"Fear not!" yelled the captain, with eyes wide in glee,
"All storms bring good tales, come raise up your tea!"

The lightning struck bright, oh, what a delight,
As the crew stumbled 'round like a comical sight.
They danced with their flasks, seeking joy in the squall,
While the waves tossed their ship like a carnival ball.

"Let the tempest bring bonkers!" they all raised a shout,
As sharks joined the party, swirling about.
The clouds they did rumble, but laughter rang clear,
In the face of the chaos, they breathlessly cheered.

So when storms start to brew and you feel quite annoyed,
Remember those sailors in tempest deployed.
With a pinch of good humor, laugh out loud with glee,
For the wild, crazy sea is a party, you see!

Nautical Notes

A fish with a hat sang a jingle so nice,
As dolphins joined in, it sounded precise.
With bubbles for rhythm and waves for the beat,
They twirled and they laughed, not caring for heat.

A squid played the keys on a piano of coral,
While turtles tapped toes, involving a maural.
"Let's dance till we drop," the seabeds did cry,
As jellyfish glowed like a disco ball high.

"Underwater boogie," a starfish declared,
Flipping his limbs, while no one else cared.
"Oh, let's throw a party!" cried seahorses bright,
And all of the fish zoomed in with delight.

So if you plunge deep and find yourself here,
Join in on the fun, let go of your fear.
For beneath all the waves, there's a tune to be heard,
As life teems with laughter, it's truly absurd!

The Sea's Timeless Ballad

A fish in a tux, quite a sight,
Dancing with jelly, what a delight.
He spins with pride, takes a bow,
Who knew fish could party like this now?

Seagulls squawk in their finest attire,
Complaining loudly, they never tire.
With sandwiches hoarded, the picnic is grand,
While crabs plot their heist in the soft, warm sand.

A starfish reclines, shades on its eyes,
While barnacles gossip under the sky.
The tide rolls in, but nobody cares,
For the underwater revelry that declares!

Oh, how the barnacles love to chime,
Counting the ways they waste their time.
With barnacle bands and dancing whales,
Every wave carries their giggles and tales!

Ebb and Flow of Forgotten Tales

Once a crab lost its favorite shoe,
It asked the clams for a clue or two.
They hid in their shells, giggling loud,
While the crab waved its claws, feeling quite proud.

An octopus juggles pearls with flair,
While mermaids sit brushing their long, flowing hair.
They chat about sailors who once took a plunge,
How they mistook seashells for treasure and funge.

The tide whispers secrets, both silly and sweet,
As dolphins play tricks and do flips with their feet.
A big whale swims by, tries to tell a joke,
But his belly gets tickled, he starts to choke.

With fish in bow ties, they prance and they play,
As barnacles laugh, seizing the day.
The sea's old tales ripple, both wild and free,
In this playful kingdom beneath the deep sea!

Shadows of the Shipwreck's Silence

Shipwrecks moan like an old, creaky bed,
As the fish search the rooms where lost dreams tread.
A parrotfish squawks at the rusty old door,
Inviting the octopus for a fun-filled tour.

Treasure chests filled with soggy old socks,
Pirate ghosts argue like children in blocks.
With a glimmer of gold gleaming under the light,
They bicker and squabble over who's had the right.

A clam opens wide to share a grand pun,
While the sea turtles wonder if it's all fun.
The shadows might dance, but they trip on the past,
As the laughter echoes, a shipwreck's webcast.

They tell ghostly tales, still stuck in their phase,
Of centuries drifting in salty sea haze.
While fishy fish giggle, with shimmer and glee,
By the shadows of memories lost in the sea.

The Soundtrack of Distant Horizons

A dolphin's high note swings through the blue,
With gulls on backup, a feathery crew.
They belt out a tune that's catchy and bright,
While crabs do the cha-cha, it's quite a sight!

Seaweed shimmies like dancers on stage,
As starfish snap selfies, it's all the rage.
With snappy rhythms, the ocean's alive,
Where sea creatures gather, and merriment thrives.

Each wave carries laughter, the pulses and beats,
Octopus DJs spin lines on the streets.
With conch shells blown like trumpets of old,
The ocean's a dance floor where stories unfold.

From coral enclaves to deep ocean's roar,
The soundtrack keeps playing, forevermore.
For who needs silence, when fun's on the tide,
In this watery world, let's all take a ride!

Underwater Refrain

Fish in tuxedos dance with flair,
Seaweed sways without a care.
Crabs in rhythm, click and clack,
While jellyfish float, it's a disco attack.

Mermaids giggle, tails a-swish,
They sing to whales, that's their wish.
An octopus plays the ukulele,
Dancing round coral, looking quite haily.

Sea cucumbers lose their groove,
Trying hard just to improve.
Starfish join in with a clap,
Enjoying life, in a sea gap.

The seashells chuckle, glee in sound,
As seagulls dance, spinning around.
Bubbles pop in tune so sweet,
Underwater parties, can't be beat.

Waves in Perfect Unison

Waves waltz in a splashy line,
Seagulls chat, oh, how they whine.
Surfboards try to surf the breeze,
While clams argue, saying, "Please!"

A dolphin flips, and lands a twist,
While crabs prepare their own ruckus.
Seashells cheer, on the sidelines bright,
As fish throw a splashy water fight.

Mermen grumble, stuck in place,
Wishing for a little more space.
The tide rolls in with a cheerful grin,
Inviting all to join the din.

With every push, the sea does sing,
Creating tunes like a playground swing.
A frothy laugh, a bubbly tune,
As dolphins dance 'neath a sunlit moon.

The Siren's Calling

Siren's voice just can't be missed,
Draws in sailors, oh, what a twist!
"Come join us!" they cheer with glee,
But really, it's just a crab party!

With mermaids flipping, hair a-froth,
They're practicing moves from the dance-off.
Caught in their antics, ships sway and rock,
While the horizon begs, "Please just dock!"

Tangled nets and fishnets fall,
While seahorses perform a ball.
Hiccups from laughter echo wide,
As whales break free from decorum's tide.

The sirens wink, their plans a-foil,
Inviting sailors to their spoil.
Yet everyone knows it's all just fun,
In their watery world, beneath the sun.

Resounding Shores

Footprints in sand, a giggle or two,
As kids pretend they're surfing the blue.
A wave rolls in with a playful shout,
And sandcastles crumble, there's no doubt.

A crab with shades, looking cool,
Stumbles on rocks, that's quite the fool!
Seagulls swoop, their jokes untold,
Pulling on strings, they're bold and bold.

The tide rushes in with a friendly tease,
"Catch me if you can, I'm a slippery breeze!"
The sun sets low, the laughter remains,
Echoing joy in the brilliant refrains.

As night falls, the beach gets still,
But dreams of waves give life a thrill.
In the whispers of surf and sand so fine,
Life's a funny dance, and oh, how it shines!

Reflections in the Deep

A fish in a tux, it's quite a sight,
Twirling around, oh what a delight.
Seahorses dance, wearing crowns made of sea,
They giggle and chatter, just like you and me.

Shells hold secrets, tales of the blue,
One crabs sings opera, oh what a view!
Starfish throw parties, with sand as the floor,
But octopuses juggle, and still want more!

Mussels on bicycles race through the tide,
While dolphins sip lattes, oh, what a ride!
In this silly world where the waves knock and play,
Life's just a splash, come laugh the day away.

Notes from the Abyss

Deep down below, where the funny fish swim,
A clownfish named Bert loves to sing on a whim.
With a ukulele made from a coral flute,
He serenades shrimp in their shiny green suits.

Anemones giggle, their tickles so sweet,
As turtles on skateboards roll past with great heat.
Crabs in sunglasses strut on the sand,
Waving to seaweed, the coolest in the land.

Jellyfish float by in their jelly-like haze,
Practicing dance moves that will amaze!
With a flip and a twist, they swirl and they sway,
Underwater ballet, come join the bouquet!

The Windswept Harmonies

Seagulls are singing, oh what a tune,
With beaks full of chips and a beach ball to moon.
They squawk out ballads, a raucous affair,
While crabs keep the time with their pinchers in air.

Kites in the sky just can't help but flail,
While jellybeans plop, like fish in a sail.
The wind whistles back with a giggle and song,
As laughter and waves together dance along.

Sunbathers chuckle at the waves' playful splashes,
Umbrellas turn over like dramatic crashes.
But all through the chaos, the fun never stops,
As nature's grand concert just hops and just pops!

Songs Carried by the Gulls

The gulls swoop down, with a joke or a pun,
Dropping off seaweed like it's fresh out of fun.
With raucous laughter echoing in grace,
They're hosting a feast, with a splash and a chase.

A walrus in shades joins the party below,
Blowing bubbles like he's putting on a show.
Guacamole made from kelp, what a spread!
While the crabs do a setback on their tiny legs ahead.

Frogs surf on logs as they float by the fleet,
Shouting, "Don't sink, or you're stuck in your seat!"
Seahorses giggling, their tails in a twirl,
In this fun, wavy world, come give it a whirl!

The Water's Wistful Whispers

Waves chat in goofy glee,
Bubbles tickle toes, you see.
Crabs doing dances, quite the show,
Fish with funny hats in tow.

Seagulls swoop, make silly calls,
While surfers wipe out, take the falls.
The tide hums tunes, high and low,
As seaweed dances, putting on a show.

Sandcastles built, then washed away,
Shells gossip secrets, come what may.
A dolphin flips, sends laughs around,
In this watery circus, joy is found.

Under the surface, bubbles burst,
Whales telling jokes, quenching thirst.
The currents giggle, playful and spry,
In this realm where laughter can fly.

Chorus of the Clifftop

Atop the cliffs, the breeze sings loud,
With salty jokes that thrill the crowd.
A seagull slips on a slimy rock,
While crabs all gather to watch the clock.

Tide pools sparkle, a funny sight,
As fish flip-flop, in pure delight.
Boom! A wave laughs, splashes all,
And seaweed waves, having a ball.

The sun winks down, wearing shades so cool,
While surfers tumble, breaking every rule.
The horizon grins, a cheeky tease,
As dolphins race, dancing with ease.

Crisp air carries giggles, wild and free,
Like secrets shared by a happy sea.
The shore's alive, a joyous play,
Where laughs and splashes rule the day.

Dreams Cradled by the Sea

Napping on a float, dreams take flight,
With jellyfish bobbing in pure delight.
Seashells whisper tales of old,
Of mermaids who danced, bold and gold.

Starfish grinning, a quirky crew,
As crabs perform in a grand review.
Waves tickle toes, a playful tease,
Beach balls bouncing, easy to please.

Surfers chatting with the passing clouds,
While seagulls squawk, attracting crowds.
In this world, where laughter flows,
Dreams are cradled in seafoam prose.

Every splash brings a chuckle and cheer,
As the ocean whispers, "Come hang out here!"
The sun sets low, painting the scene,
In this watery dream, where fun is queen.

The Melodic Mosaic of Mornings

Mornings burst with colors bold,
As waves roll in with stories told.
A pelican plops, then takes a dive,
While fishy friends jump, feeling alive.

Coffee brews while the tide sings soft,
Sandcastles tumble, giving a scoff.
A beach ball flies; oh what a sight,
As laughter echoes, pure delight.

The sun peeks up, a shy debut,
With seagulls cracking jokes—who knew?
Waves tap-dance, a rhythm so fine,
As beachgoers sway, enjoying the shine.

From dawn to dusk, the fun won't cease,
Waves and giggles, a comic piece.
In this joyful symphony, spirits soar,
As every morning brings laughter to shore.

Tidal Dreams

When waves crash down with a splish and a splash,
Seagulls squawk, in their sassy stashed stash.
Fish wear hats and dance in the tide,
While crabs do the cha-cha, oh what a ride!

Mermaids giggle at jellyfish pranks,
Each bubble bursts with their mischief and thanks.
A dolphin serenades with a silly grin,
As beach balls float where the fun begins!

Ocean Whispers

Starfish gossip of the sandcastle king,
While octopuses juggle, it's quite the thing!
A clam shouts funny tales to a curious whale,
As plankton tell jokes, they never fail.

Nudibranchs dressed in colors so bright,
Sass on the coral, oh what a sight!
Seashells laugh as the tide comes to tickle,
In this underwater riddle, we giggle and wiggle!

Harmony of the Driftwood

Driftwood plays tunes on the sandy shore,
As crabs hold a concert, who could ask for more?
Seashells rattle, they form a great band,
With laughter echoing across the wet land.

Barnacles boast of their sticky success,
While fish dress in ties, oh what a finesse!
A dance of the waves, oh what a delight,
As sea cucumbers groove into the night!

The Call of the Abyssal Depths

Deep down below where the sea is quite dark,
The anglerfish flaunts his luminescent spark.
Octopi tell tales with a twist and a spin,
While lanternfish laugh, let the fun begin!

A parrotfish grins as he munches on coral,
And the sea urchins share jokes with a moral.
The depths are alive with giggles and glee,
As the mysteries of laughter float wild and free!

Reverie Among Coral Reefs

In the reef where the colors can tickle your nose,
Clownfish frolic while sea turtles pose.
A pufferfish giggles as he puffs out wide,
While anemones sway, dance a joyful ride.

Coral crabs play peek-a-boo in their hide,
As sunsets paint canvases, nature's pride.
With each splash and swirl, laughter takes flight,
In this whimsical world where sea dreams ignite!

Voices of the Rolling Waves

Waves crash in a bubbly dance,
Seagulls dive with quite the prance.
Fish wearing hats, what a sight!
Even crabs join in the plight.

Starfish telling tales at sea,
"Don't get sand in your cup of tea!"
Jellyfish doing wiggly tricks,
While sea turtles munch on sticks.

The sun joins in, a radiant grin,
"Make sure to laugh, let the fun begin!"
Mermaids giggle, spritzing spray,
As they splash about in the lovely bay.

Oh, the sea is a show of glee,
With antics that make you shout, "Yippee!"
So grab a float and join the spree,
In this funny world of wild jubilee.

A Canvas of Nautical Dreams

Underwater paintings swirl with glee,
A dolphin paints a smile, can't you see?
Paintbrushes made from kelp and foam,
Creating colors where fish roam.

Octopuses juggling seaweed balls,
While crabs play chess on coral walls.
Starfish on drums keep the beat,
As fishy dancers tap their feet.

A whale splashes with a grand display,
Making waves that carry dreams away.
The canvas shifts with giggles bright,
As sea creatures dance into the night.

This colorful sea is quite a sight,
With laughter echoing day and night!
So let your dreams set sail like boats,
On a canvas that the ocean promotes.

Waves Whisper Melodies

In the shallows, whispers fly,
The salty breeze, a laughter high.
Waves that tickle toes on sand,
As beach balls soar at a kid's command.

Crabs conducting with tiny claws,
While dolphins leap, they earn applause.
Seagulls squawk in a comical tune,
As they dance below a quirky moon.

The shore sings softly, "Come and play,
Let's make this a joyous day!"
The tide rushes in with a cheer,
As fish wear spectacles, "Oh dear!"

Each wave a note, each splash a song,
In this funny world where we belong.
Surfing laughter on the crest,
With waves that invite us to jest.

Currents of Echoing Dreams

Currents swirl with giggly dreams,
Fish gossip loud, or so it seems.
They share secrets of seaweed snack,
While starfish give a ticklish whack.

A clam snaps shut, "Quiet, please!"
As shrimp break into a silly sneeze.
Jellybeans in jelly fish, oh wow!
The underwater party says, "Take a bow!"

The tide plots stars in ink and teal,
With waves that spin a grand reveal.
Anemones sway, wearing hats,
While sea cucumbers dance with spats.

Currents of laughter bubble up,
In this fun-filled sea, let's raise a cup!
So dive right in, don't be shy,
Join this party, oh my, oh my!

Harmonies of the Distant Dawn

Seagulls squawk a silly tune,
While crabs dance like there's a full moon.
Waves laugh and splash in a swirling race,
Fish giggle as they flip in a watery space.

A starfish sports a bright red tie,
Sipping seaweed green tea nearby.
Shells gossip in the salty breeze,
All while jellyfish float with such ease.

The pelicans play a game of catch,
Dropping their fish, what a crazy match!
Barnacles cling with a sticky cheer,
As the sun arrives, shining so clear.

Each splash and pop joins the harmony,
Creating waves of fun, oh so free!
With laughter that echoes through the brine,
Where every tide brings a joke so fine.

Songs of Salt and Sky

A dolphin flips with a cheeky grin,
While sea turtles glide with a flappy fin.
The clouds tickle the waves below,
As sandy toes dance in a row.

Octopuses juggle pearls and shells,
While shrimp tap dance in their tiny wells.
The breeze whispers jokes to the gulls,
As laughter floats, filling all pulls.

With each bouncy wave comes a twist and squeal,
Crabs marching like soldiers, what a surreal deal!
Kelp sways like it's had too much fun,
Under a sky that's never done.

Each splash adds a beat to the salty air,
Where sea creatures gather without a care.
Laughter echoes from shore to shore,
In this silly place, who could ask for more?

Whispers of the Wandering Wind

The wind carries tales of teasing shells,
As waves romp around like playful elves.
Seagulls mimic the sound of a song,
Chasing each other all day long.

Starfish argue over who'll take the lead,
While little minnows plot a speedy deed.
The breeze pulls pranks, flicking hats away,
As the sand wishes it could join the fray.

Clams giggle as they pinching retreat,
When a rogue wave plays a comical repeat.
The sun beams down with a wink and a glance,
Encouraging all to join in the dance.

The tides are stitched with laughter and fun,
Creating a symphony, second to none.
With every burst of bubbling cheer,
Nature's antics, we'll always hold dear.

Fluid Footsteps on the Sand

Footprints vanish with a cheeky grin,
As waves tickle toes with a splashy spin.
A crab scuttles sideways, what a sight,
Making fun of hikers with all its might.

A picnic blanket flops in crazy winds,
While seagulls swoop down for snacks on whims.
Shells hum little tunes as the tide rolls in,
While dolphins propose a synchronized spin.

The horizon giggles with cotton-candy clouds,
As kids chase the waves and shout out loud.
Each new splash sends ripples of glee,
In this quirky place where joy feels free.

So follow the track of the playful tide,
Where laughter and fun are our faithful guide.
Every grain of sand holds a whimsical cheer,
In the land where joy is always near!

The Call of the Tidal Heart

The waves are laughing, can you hear?
They splash and dance without a fear.
A crab wears slippers, oh so bright,
While seagulls sing in pure delight.

Flip-flops fly with every wave,
As starfish cheer, they're feeling brave.
The octopus, a master chef,
Makes pasta from the ocean's left.

A dolphin dives, it sneezes loud,
Sending bubbles to the crowd.
With seaweed wigs, they twirl and spin,
Oh, what a party to be in!

So bring your jokes, your silly hat,
We'll laugh along with every splat.
For where the waters twist and swirl,
Life's a giggle in a swirl!

Sea Shanties in Soliloquy

Up on deck, the pirates sing,
With wooden legs and cloth for bling.
They belt out tunes, a funny sight,
While fish do tango in the light.

A parrot squawks, "Let's sail away!"
But gets distracted by the bay.
With snacks of jelly, they all feast,\nOh, what a ruckus, to say the least!

A crab drops anchor with a grin,
While whales waltz, let's join in!
The tides are swaying, full of cheer,
The captain's hat just flew in here!

So sing along, don't miss a beat,
The sea is calling, oh so sweet.
In salty air, our hearts ignite,
With shanties swirling in the night!

Moonlit Murmurs at Dusk

The moon comes out, it winks and sighs,
As fish put on a grand disguise.
With googly eyes and sparkly scales,
They dance on waves, dodging gales.

A dolphin dons a velvet cape,
And makes a splash with every scrape.
The jellyfish glow like disco balls,
As laughter bounces off the walls.

Seagulls croak their own weird tunes,
While clams play cards beneath the moons.
A crab declares, "I'm king tonight!"
As everyone joins in delight.

So let's all gather, hand in fin,
To laugh and joke and spin again.
The night is young, the fun won't cease,
With moonlit laughs, we find our peace!

The Ripple of Forgotten Tales

Once a fish dreamt he could fly,
He tried to jump, oh my, oh my!
He flopped around, then hit a wave,
And landed on a friendly knave.

A whale tells tales of ancient days,
Of treasure maps and pirate ways.
But every plot twist makes them snore,
As they roll over with a roar.

Sandcastles crumble in the breeze,
As crabs march by with utmost ease.
They chant of battles won so grand,
With tiny swords made from the sand.

So join the tales where laughter's found,
In every ripple, joy's abound.
With every wave that comes ashore,
Let's spin our stories forevermore!

Ballad of the Rolling Surf

Waves crash like a band on tour,
Each splash a giggle, that's for sure.
Seagulls squawk their sassy tunes,
While surfers balance on the dunes.

Shells dance like dancers in the sand,
With flip-flops flopping, not quite planned.
A crab does the cha-cha, side to side,
While kids jump in, their joy won't hide.

The sun sets down, a stage so bright,
As dolphins leap with pure delight.
Don't let the tide sweep you away,
Or you might be lost till the next day!

With every wave, there's laughter loud,
The beach is a party for every crowd.
So grab your floaties, here we go,
In the rolling surf, there's always a show!

Chants of the Seafarers

In boats that bob like corks afloat,
We sing some shanties in every note.
The fish are listening, winks and glares,
As we chant quirky tunes for our hares.

A sailor slips, he grabs a net,
And out pops a fish, all soggy and wet.
To catch our breath, we all can't wait,
As he tells a tale that's quite first-rate.

With hooks and lines, we twirl and spin,
The crab gives nods with a silly grin.
"Fish not dinner!" we shout for fun,
As everyone yells, "I won, I won!"

The sails are flapping, the wind a blast,
Making our future look quite the cast.
We chug along, a crew so brave,
As the sea laughs back, soaked in our rave.

Melodic Mists of Morning

The sun peeks wide with a sleepy yawn,
While dolphins twirl at the break of dawn.
Waves whisper secrets in soft, sweet mist,
As beachgoers line up, none can resist.

A coffee spills on a sunburned leg,
While kiddos giggle, others beg.
With morning tides, the sea throws a party,
Convincing longboards to join, quite hearty.

Seagulls swoop low, dive-bombing for fries,
While surfboards compete for the biggest surprise.
But one flip-flop goes sailing away,
Leaving its pair for a comical play.

As mists lift slowly, a smile blooms bright,
With every ripple, it feels just right.
So raise a toast with your morning brew,
The beach is alive, and it's all about you!

Secrets in the Seafoam

In frothy whispers, tales unfold,
Of treasure maps and pirates bold.
The seafoam giggles, tickling toes,
As the shore reveals what nobody knows.

A flip-flop army, they march in line,
Seeking the sun, it's party time!
With buckets and shovels, they scoot across,
While crabs throw parties at great, great cost.

Seashells hold secrets, or so we hear,
Of mermaids singing, oh-so-clear.
But when we ask, they just roll their eyes,
And dive below, oh how they despise!

So let's raise a laugh to the sea's great fun,
As sandcastles crumble when the day is done.
With every bubble, there's something to find,
In the whimsical world of the ocean's mind.

Serenade in Swell and Break

In waves that dance like silly clowns,
Seagulls squawk in feathered gowns.
They swoop and dive, splash and play,
Making a mess of our picnic day.

A crab in shades, he struts around,
Claiming the sand, he's king, he's crowned.
With every wave, he scuttles back,
In this fishy tale, he's the main act.

The sunbeam surfboards, rides the crest,
While dolphins giggle, they're doing their best!
The tide takes a bow, then swells with laughter,
Creating joy, ever after.

With flip-flops flung and laughter shared,
The antics here are wildly aired.
In this watery realm, silly and spry,
We laugh with the waves as they splash by.

The Singing Sand

The grains of gold with voices bright,
Whispering jokes in the warm daylight.
Tickled by toes, they slide and swirl,
Dancing like silly kids in a whirl.

Wind plays the flute, a sea breeze sings,
Each note a splash, oh what fun it brings!
A seashell chorus, oh how they strive,
To harmonize in this sandy jive.

"Hey there, dunes, don't get too proud,
We're the sandy stars, we're loud and loud!"
With castles built and laughter loud,
The singing grains form a crazy crowd.

So waltz with the tide, don't be so grand,
Join the parade through the singing sand.
With each funny note of chorus and cheer,
The beach is the best place to lounge and leer.

Breezes of Forgotten Sea Stories

A breeze from the past tickles our ears,
Whispering tales from salty years.
A fish in a hat, quite out of time,
Claims he can rap, his rhythm's a crime.

Seaweed's tangled in laughter and plays,
Each strand a pro in hilarious ways.
A clam's got a secret, or so it seems,
Whispers of treasure in the sailors' dreams.

The currents giggle, they twist and bend,
Making fun of their watery friends.
With a splash and a froth, they mimic the past,
Those breezes blow tales, oh, so vast.

So share a laugh with the breeze today,
Let the stories roll in, come what may.
For in the vast blue, humor's not shy,
Every wave and whisper begs you to try.

Abyssal Melancholy

In depths so deep, where few have tread,
Lives a fish with a crown, who's feeling dread.
He says, "Why swim when I can just float?
All these other fish? They just gloat!"

The octopus juggles, but stumbles too,
With eight wiggly arms, can't know what to do!
"Who knew being funny would be a test?
I just wanted to show off my best!"

A whale sings low, with a woeful tone,
"Underwater blues, I'm so alone!
Why must my songs be filled with sorrow?
Laughter's a treasure, I'll borrow!"

But bubbles burst forth, full of glee,
The abyss teems with humor, wait and see!
For even in depths, where shadows persist,
A chuckle can ripple, oh, how it twists!

Chimes of the Cresting Waves

The seagulls squawk in harmony,
While fish wear hats and dance with glee,
A crab plays jazz on a water flute,
And dolphins join in, oh what a hoot!

A turtle tries to moonwalk too,
But slips and lands in a sea of blue,
With jellyfish as the audience,
They all laugh loud, oh what a suspense!

The waves clap hands like a cheering crowd,
As sea urchins jest, feeling quite proud,
While corals sway to the ocean's beat,
In this watery world, life's quite a treat!

Stars above share their bright applause,
For starfish who have four left feet paws,
As tides retreat and the creatures cheer,
The symphony plays with nothing to fear!

The Tune of the Timeless Tide

Barnacles sing in funky chairs,
While octopuses change their pairs,
The snail, quite slow, is a solid fan,
And sea cucumbers join the jam!

A clownfish tells a joke so funny,
About a whale who lost his money,
The tide roars laughter, splashing about,
While plankton giggle and swim without doubt!

The sea horse spins, looking quite spry,
As sea lions bark, oh my, oh my!
They dance and twirl as the waves combine,
Creating a mashup that's simply divine!

Bubbles pop in rhythm and time,
As everything sways to the watery rhyme,
With shells as instruments, all play along,
In the deep where the merry songs throng!

Chorus of the Nautical Night

At midnight, fishes throw a grand ball,
With snappy outfits that rise and fall,
A pufferfish tries to fit in tight,
But keeps puffing and causing a fright!

Kraken's food delivery is quite bizarre,
Bringing seaweed pies and bacon from afar,
While mermaids hum tunes from ages past,
Their fishy friends join in, having a blast!

A funny shark wears glasses too big,
He smiles wide, showing his toothy jig,
With a flashlight beam, he leads the fun,
Making waves with laughter, oh what a run!

The stars above wink, knowing the score,
As turtles groove on the ocean floor,
Each wave carries joy, echoes and sighs,
In this night of laughter beneath the skies!

Voices of the Vast

Clams gossip about the latest trends,
While crabs do the cha-cha with their friends,
The fish have flippers that sparkle and glow,
As the seaweed waltzes to and fro!

A snail spins tales of high seas adventures,
But drags his foot, losing all conjectures,
With conch shell trumpets leading the way,
Oysters all hum, come what may!

Anemones sway, looking quite grand,
As they throw a party on the sand,
With sea snails serving drinks made of brine,
The merriment flows like a good bottle of wine!

So here's to laughter, in every wave,
As life in the deep, we joyfully pave,
With tunes and giggles, great memories cast,
In this quirky world, where fun is steadfast!

Serenade of the Sea

A fish in a tux, he's quite the sight,
Dancing with crabs every Friday night.
They waltz on the waves, such a quirky crew,
With jellyfish friends who glow in the blue.

The seagulls laugh with their feathered flair,
Counting the shells in salty air.
"Why did the octopus cross the tide?"
"To ink a message, let's take a ride!"

A whale sings deep, with a bubble pop,
While dolphins tap dance, never stop.
They spin in glee, with a splashy cheer,
In murky waters, they've no time for fear.

So here's to the waves, in their playful song,
Where fish find fun and we all belong.
With laughter so loud, and splashes so free,
Life's a beach, come swim with me!

The Blue Horizon's Echo

Upon waves that giggle, the sun blinks bright,
Fish wear their shades, what a silly sight!
Seashells gossip like a chatty crowd,
"Who wore it best?" they're all very proud.

The crabs tell jokes, with claws raised high,
"Ever seen a lobster learn to fly?"
They wheeze with laughter as the tide takes a break,
While seahorses skate like it's a big lake.

Anemones sway, they steal the show,
In their flouncy skirts, they put on a glow.
"Join us for tea!" they beckon and plead,
With tea made of seaweed, just take heed!

Each wave a pun, each current a jest,
In this watery world, we're truly blessed.
So splash in the fun, don't let it flee,
Life's better with bubbles, just wait and see!

Symphony Beneath the Surface

Down below, where the seaweed sways,
A clam's got rhythm, in quirky ways.
He's playing a tune on a worn-out shell,
While starfish sway, and the crabs rebel.

Turtles ride bass, in a slow, cool groove,
While bubbles dance to the beat, so smooth.
"Have you heard the one about the crab?"
He lost his pinch, it was quite the blab!

A pufferfish sings with a voice so grand,
But then puffs up, can't quite make a stand.
While clownfish chuckle, no playing it straight,
It's a fishy affair, but never too late.

So join in the orchestra, let's all partake,
Beneath the surface, there's laughter to make.
With every bubble and every little splash,
The ocean's alive, let's have a blast!

Tides of Timeless Harmony

In the frothy brine, there's a raucous cheer,
Sea cucumbers giggle, they've no fear.
With a flip and a flop, they boast their moves,
While fish sing songs, in their groovy grooves.

A manta ray slides by, in a tux it seems,
Waltzing through water, shattering dreams.
"Have you seen my dance?" it asks with glee,
Flipping through currents, just wait and see!

Sardines form a band, with a rhythmic thrum,
Marching in schools, how do they come?
The shrimp throw a party, cranking up the dial,
In this silly sea, they're dressing with style.

So let's raise a fin, and toast to the waves,
For laughter and joy in these watery caves.
With every tide, let our spirits be light,
In this sea of wonders, the future feels bright!

Dances of the Deep

In the deep, fish do twirl,
A crab does the twist in a whirl.
Seaweed sways, in ballet attire,
While a dolphin's joke inspires a choir.

Starfish clap with their five tiny hands,
As a clam makes art with ocean sands.
A parrotfish laughs, a real jokester,
Says, 'Who needs land? We're the best coastal poster!'

With bubbles popping, the fun won't cease,
In this deep dance, all find their peace.
Octopus juggles, a true sight to see,
In the watery ball, come dance with me!

So, if you're down, take a dive with glee,
Join in the fun, be wild and free.
Under the waves, laughter prevails,
Where silliness thrives beneath wet veils.

Lullabies of the Salted Breeze

The seagulls croon in a quirky tone,
A fishy ballad, you're not alone.
The waves hum tunes, with squeals and splashes,
While barnacles join in with their gentle clashes.

Whales sing softly, oh what a range,
'Tell us a joke,'—the dolphins exclaim.
The snoozing shrimp, in a sleepy haze,
Start giggling softly in salted rays.

Turtles nod off, with a chuckle or two,
In their dreams, they dance, the ocean's crew.
Bubbles explode into chuckles afloat,
As crabby puns echo from a cozy boat.

So let the sea rock you, giggle and sway,
To the silly songs that will brighten your day.
With laughter that bubbles like sweet ocean spritz,
You'll find joy in the sea, no matter the twists.

Surging Rhythms of the Coast

The coast beats a rhythm, a silly parade,
With waves that stumble, their dance mislaid.
Surfboards wobble, in goofy glee,
While the sandcastles chuckle, 'Oh, look at me!'

Sand crabs scuttle in a frantic flow,
Practicing moves like they're on a show.
The tide pulls back, they parade like fools,
'We're the dance troupe of the ocean's schools!'

Seashells clink, like tiny triangles,
As the dolphins flip, they share their tangles.
With a splash and a giggle, they steal the show,
The rhythm of surf gives us endless flow.

So sway with the waves, let laughter explode,
In the soggy disco, we lighten the load.
From sunrise to sunset, it's a joyous coast,
Where the beats meet the tide, we dance with a boast!

Beneath the Celestial Waves

Beneath the waves, where giggles abound,
A fishy comedian reigns with no sound.
With a wink and a flip, they pull a prank,
While a sneaky eel swims in a prankster tank.

Stars twinkle above in a watery plight,
While a starfish shouts, 'I bear this night!'
Sea urchins chuckle, pokey yet sweet,
As jellyfish wiggle to their own little beat.

Anemones dance, just waving along,
With a grin, they sing a seaweed song.
The moon's silver glow makes creatures rejoice,
In the depths where the sea gives them a voice.

So come on, dear friends, dive down below,
Where sunshine and laughter make ebb and flow.
In this warm underwater, styled so spry,
Life's a deep chuckle beneath a big sky.

Ebbing Melodies of the Moon

The waves dance like a clumsy cat,
Splashing water on my favorite hat.
Seagulls squawk in a chorus of cheer,
While I try to catch a fish with a beer.

The tide pulls me in, then pushes me out,
My boat's tied to nothing, oh what a clout!
A mermaid waves from her sunken chair,
"Come join me for tea, if you dare!"

Flip-flops float by on a journey of their own,
With barnacles hitching a ride, how they've grown!
I take a dive, but what do I find?
A jellyfish tickles, oh how unrefined!

As evening falls, the gulls take to bed,
With all of the snacks that they gleaned and led.
I hum a tune with the stars shining bright,
"Catch me a crab!" I call out in spite!

A Cadence of Currents

The currents swirl like a dance-off gone wrong,
With fish auditioning, all singing a song.
One thought he could conga, slipped and went splat,
Now he's sharing a laugh with a nearby brat.

Trains of seaweed float by, like fanciful trains,
While I try to recall my old rock and rains.
A walrus in shades gives a wink and says,
"Surf's up tomorrow, we'll catch the big waves!"

My bucket of crabs holds an unexpected prize,
A pint-sized lobster in a fake disguise.
He points to the crabs, declares with a grin,
"Your dance moves are hopeless, let my party begin!"

Fish fumble through bubbles, all in a rush,
To join the parade in an aquatic crush.
As laughter echoes across the whole bay,
I shout, "Oh dear, will I join in today?"

Lyrical Longing on the Shore

Footprints in the sand lead me to the sea,
Where a crab plays the drums, oh what glee!
He's got a conch shell, acting like a sax,
And I can't help but join in with some wax.

Turtles tap dance, wearing tiny top hats,
And dolphins dive in with glittery spats.
The rhythmic tides sing of nights gone by,
As I try to improvise, looking quite spry.

The tide rolls in with a splashy report,
As fish open up like they're on for support.
A birthday bash for a whale without fear,
With streamers of kelp, it's quite a grand cheer!

Ahoy! I sip from my coconut cup,
As the sea plays the tunes, we all try to sup.
Who knew that the sea could throw such a bash?
With laughter like waves, oh what a splash!

Ballads Beneath the Surface

Beneath the waves, a party unfolds,
With turtles and octopuses daring the bold.
A clam plays the piano, made out of shells,
While the fish form a chorus, and oh, how it swells.

I dive for a glimpse of this rhythmic delight,
And see jellyfish twirling in outfits so bright.
They drift through the water like elegant gowns,
In a frolicsome ballet, never wear frowns.

Anemones sway to the jazz of the night,
While starfish throw popcorn and laugh in delight.
"Join us!" they call, with a wink of their rays,
As I dance with the tides, lost in the sway.

With bubbles and giggles, fun reigns supreme,
As sea creatures gather to live out their dream.
In the world down below, where the silly is king,
I'll waltz through the waves and just let my heart sing!

Soliloquy of the Deep Blue

A fish in a tux, oh what a sight,
Practicing steps in the moon's soft light.
He slips and he slides, what a silly scene,
Dancing with jelly in a waltz so keen.

The currents all giggle, they can't help but sway,
While an octopus joins in, with ink on display.
A crab does the cha-cha, oh, what a fun show,
As starfish applaud in their five-digit glow.

An eel tells a joke, it's a bit of a shock,
Tangled in seaweed, he's locked in a block.
But laughter erupts from the clams on the floor,
Who knew that the ocean could chuckle galore!

So here in the deep, with glee we shall plunge,
In the realm of the waves, where we dance and we lunge.
The joys of the water, both silly and bright,
Keep singing and laughing, till we say goodnight.

A Song Carried by the Wind

The breeze tickles seagulls as they fly around,
Chasing their shadows, what a sight they've found!
A crab with a hat croaks a tune so absurd,
While a clam taps its shell, making beats unheard.

The breeze, still laughing, pushes forth with a shout,
As a dolphin flips high, and a tuna spins out.
They gather for concerts beneath the bright sun,
Each wave plays a note, oh, the harmony's fun!

A turtle forgets where he left his keys,
While nudging a fish, "Swim left, if you please!"
But the fish just rolls over, a giggle escapes,
As lanternfish wink in their shimmering shapes.

So dance with the waves, let your cares drift away,
The ocean sings songs that make hearts want to play.
With laughter and rhythm, we all join the blend,
Together with the tides, let the merriment end!

Reflections in a Saltwater Mirror

In a seaweed mirror, a crab sees his face,
Wonders why he's the silliest in the whole place.
His friend the clownfish jokes, "You're quite the star!"
While a shrimp nearby laughs, holding a big jar.

The reflections twist funny, as waves ripple by,
A squidding squawk rises, and seagulls all fly.
"Why don't jellyfish dance?" asks a curious fin,
"They do it in slow-mo, always ready to spin!"

A whale hums a tune, deep and wide as can be,
While munching on krill with a side of the sea.
But he gets quite distracted by plankton's sweet groove,
And starts doing the twist with a jellyfish move.

So gaze at the surface, where antics unfold,
With laughter that bubbles, a joy to behold.
In the saltwater mirror, all creatures take part,
In the great, goofy dance that ignites every heart!

Rhapsody of the Wandering Whales

Two whales in a ballet, they leap and they dive,
Waltzing through bubbles, where dreams come alive.
With splashes of laughter that echo the sea,
They belt out their tunes, oh, so joyfully free!

A school of young fish join their rhythmic beat,
Twisting and twirling, they're light on their feet.
But a clownfish shouts, "Wait, what's that? A shadow!"
It's just a big sunfish, moving oh so slow.

A turtle slides in, wearing sunglasses bright,
Says, "Where's the party? I'm here for the night!"
With jokes filled with giggles, and tales from afar,
They share in the fun, under the light of the star.

So wander the waves, sing songs loud and clear,
The rhapsody carries through waters we cheer.
With giggles and splashes, we all join along,
In the great, endless cheer that is humankind's song!

An Odyssey Beneath the Surface

Bubbles rise, fish take a peek,
A crab wearing shades plays hide and seek.
Starfish lounge, taking a rest,
While sea cucumbers are dressed at their best.

Waves tickle the sand in a ticklish dance,
A dolphin slips by, gives a cheeky glance.
Jellyfish waltz in the moonlit rays,
Riding the currents, they giggle all day.

Seashells gossip about tides and the sun,
An octopus thinks deep thoughts, oh what fun!
Fish with a sense of fashion parade,
While sea turtles grab snacks at the mermaid's arcade.

Coral reefs sparkle with a colorful glow,
And clownfish joke while they steal the show.
The underwater realm, a wild, funny scene,
Where laughter and bubbles reign supreme.

Symphony of the Sea Foam

Foam frolics and dances, a bubbly delight,
Seagulls waddle around, looking for a bite.
A fish with a hat, sings a jolly tune,
While crabs keep the beat with the waves' gentle swoon.

Rays of sunshine bounce off the blue,
As starfish cheer for the clam's silly crew.
A sea horse jigs while the waves all clap,
While barnacles tap on a barn door, what a rap!

Turtles groove slow, it's their ice cream break,
And clams sing softly for goodness' sake.
Sea urchins spin in a dizzying whirl,
Their spiky attire causing quite a swirl.

Crabs juggle shells with a wink and a grin,
A splashy parade, let the fun begin!
And through all the laughter, the foam sings along,
In this joyous splash zone, can't help but belong.

Nightfall's Lullaby on the Shore

Stars twinkle above with a mischievous gleam,
As the sea whispers secrets in a watery dream.
Crabs dance in shadows, dodging the light,
While clams snicker softly at the passing night.

Seagulls nestled, all cozy and sweet,
While the ocean's soft murmur lulls them to sleep.
The rhythm of waves hugs the sandy shore,
As sandcastles giggle, 'We wish for more!'

An old fish retells stories of glee,
Of pirates and mermaids, oh what a spree!
While seaweed sways with a rustling cheer,
And wink at the moon, they know no fear.

A wave splashes high, bubbles start to play,
As sleepy-eyed otters begin to sway.
Wrapped in the tides' soft and calming embrace,
Nightfall's a lullaby, a warm, happy place.

Secrets of the Hidden Currents

Currents swirl secrets that fish have to share,
With tales of mischief floating in the air.
A mermaid with pearls breaks into a jig,
While a whale in the back starts to boogie real big!

Octopuses whisper, but never give clues,
About treasure maps hidden in the blues.
Clams are the keepers of stories untold,
With laughter and pearls worth more than gold.

Anemones bob, dressed up for a ball,
While sea urchins decide to grow extra tall.
Starfish on stilts take a twirling spin,
While fish bet on which way the tide will begin.

Dolphins play hide and seek, jumping for joy,
Chasing their tails like a playful old boy.
As secrets and giggles mix into the foam,
In the currents of laughter, all creatures feel home.

www.ingramcontent.com/pod-product-compliance
Lightning Source LLC
Chambersburg PA
CBHW060123230426
43661CB00003B/302